THE BEST OF
CREOLE COOKING

THE BEST OF CREOLE COOKING

Published in the United Kingdom by
CENTURION BOOKS LIMITED
52 George Street, London W1H 5RF

ISBN: 0-948500-12-3

The book was designed and produced by
Centurion Design Forum, London, UK

Line drawings produced from original photographs
loaned by the American Museum in Britain

All food was prepared and photographed
at the studios of 3 Score, Atlanta, USA

Colour origination by
Pre-Press Services, Leeds, UK

Printed and bound in the United States of America

THE BEST OF
CREOLE COOKING

LES CARLOSS

CENTURION

THE BEST OF
CREOLE COOKING

My love for Creole food stems from having grown up in the South and living in Louisiana for many years. I was fortunate that my work enabled me to travel extensively through that State, thereby enabling me to sample the many diverse Creole and Cajun foods on offer. Whether I was in the heart of the Bayou country feasting on exquisite Cajun cuisine, or dining in the legendary 'institutions' in the French Quarter of New Orleans, I became intrigued with the many variations of cuisines and their unique presentations.

Indeed, I became so fascinated that I made the decision to leave the security of my long-time sales job to attend a relatively obscure, but extremely creative, cooking school in New Orleans. Here I met Bud Deslatte, whose passion for Creole cooking was similar to mine and it was not long before we started discussing the idea of opening our own restaurant with the school's Manager/Chef, Sylvia Harbin. As a result the three of us joined forces to open *Feelings Café D'Aunoy* just outside the French Quarter.

That was in 1979 and in the next fourteen years we opened a further five restaurants, *A Taste of New Orleans* (1985), *Crescent City* (1987) and *French Quarter Food Shop* (1987), all in Atlanta; and then, moving West, *Bayou Bar and Grill* (1989) and *Crawdaddy's Cafeteria* (1991) in San Diego. They were all designed as casually-elegant 'bistros' to serve reasonably priced food, prepared in the New Orleans manner. The success of the formula was proven by the regular patronage that each venue quickly established and consistently held on to.

The recipes on the following pages are a selection of the most popular traditional and unique creations served in our restaurants. Some may prove at first to be a little complicated but you'll be surprised at how many are simple to prepare. I hope you'll enjoy them and get pleasure and satisfaction by serving your family and friends some of **THE BEST OF CREOLE COOKING.**

CREOLE MUSTARD SAUCE

1 cup dry white vermouth
1 tablespoon white wine vinegar
1 tablespoon finely chopped shallot
1 teaspoon chopped tarragon
1 tablespoon finely chopped red bell pepper
1/2 cup heavy whipping cream
1 teaspoon puréed garlic
1 tablespoon Creole mustard
1 teaspoon Dijon mustard
1/2 teaspoon cayenne pepper
1/2 white pepper
salt to taste
4 ounces unsalted butter

Place the vermouth, vinegar and shallot in a saucepan and stir over a high heat until reduced to approximately 3 tablespoons. Add the tarragon, bell pepper and cream and reduce heat to medium, then add garlic, mustards, peppers and salt. Stir for 1 minute, then whisk in the butter, a tablespoon at a time, and stir for a further minute. Remove from heat and serve immediately.

CREOLE TOMATO SAUCE

4 ounces butter
1/2 cup finely chopped yellow onion
1 cup finely chopped green onion
1 cup finely chopped green bell pepper
1/4 cup finely chopped celery
2 cups chicken stock
2 cups peeled and diced tomatoes
1 teaspoon puréed garlic
2 bay leaves
1/2 teaspoon thyme
1 teaspoon paprika
1 teaspoon Louisiana hot sauce
1 teaspoon Creole seasoning
salt and pepper to taste
1 tablespoon cornstarch

Heat the butter in a pan and sauté the onions, bell pepper and celery for 5 minutes, then add the stock and all remaining ingredients, excluding the cornstarch. Bring to the boil, then reduce heat and allow to simmer for 35-40 minutes. Mix the cornstarch with 1/4 cup of water and stir into the sauce. Simmer for a further 10 minutes, then remove bay leaves and serve immediately.

SEAFOOD BUTTER SAUCE

12 medium size fresh shrimp
1/2 pound crawfish tails
8 ounces butter
2 teaspoons Creole seasoning
1/2 pound fresh lump crabmeat
1/2 cup finely chopped green onion
2 tablespoons all-purpose flour
1/2 teaspoon dried basil
1/2 teaspoon thyme
1/2 teaspoon oregano
1 teaspoon puréed garlic
1 teaspoon Worcestershire sauce
1/2 teaspoon Louisiana hot sauce

Shell and de-vein the shrimp and shell the crawfish tails. Melt 4 ounces of butter in a skillet, add the Creole seasoning, and sauté until the shrimp turns pink. Remove the shrimp, then add the remaining butter and sauté the crawfish for 5 minutes. Remove the crawfish and blend with the shrimp, then add the crabmeat and onion and combine with the other seafood. Add the flour to the pan juices and stir for 2 minutes, then add the remaining ingredients and cook for a further 3-4 minutes.

RAISIN SAUCE

³/₄ cup Coca-Cola
³/₄ cup chicken stock (see below)
³/₄ cup brown sugar
³/₄ cup raisins
2 tablespoons cornstarch

Pour the cola and stock into a saucepan, add the sugar and raisins and bring to the boil. Mix the cornstarch with a small quantity of cold water and add to the pan. Reduce to a simmer and stir until a desired consistency is achieved.

JALAPENO TARTER SAUCE

1 cup mayonnaise
¹/₄ cup sweet pickle relish
2 tablespoons finely chopped capers
¹/₄ cup finely chopped jalapeno peppers
2 tablespoons finely chopped yellow onion
¹/₄ cup finely chopped parsley
1 tablespoon horseradish
1 teaspoon dry mustard

Place all the ingredients in a mixing bowl and blend thoroughly. Refrigerate for at least 2 hours before serving.

CHICKEN STOCK

3-4 pounds chicken pieces with bones
2 large yellow onions, peeled and quartered
3-4 peeled garlic cloves
2 large carrots, sliced
3-4 broken celery ribs
celery leaves
10-12 sprigs parsley
2 bay leaves

Place all the chicken pieces in a stock and add water to cover. Bring to the boil and skim off any surface scum, then reduce heat and add all the remaining ingredients. Add more water to ensure the vegetables are covered and simmer for 3-4 hours until the liquid is reduced by half. Remove from heat and strain into sterilized containers. May be frozen.

SEAFOOD STOCK

2-3 pounds shrimp shells and heads with fish trimmings and bones
1 large yellow onion, peeled and quartered
3-4 peeled garlic cloves
2 large carrots, sliced
3-4 broken ribs of celery
celery leaves
10-12 sprigs of parsley
2 bay leaves
1 lemon, quartered
1 teaspoon cayenne pepper

Place all the seafood shells and bones in a large stockpot. Add water to cover and bring to the boil. Skim off any surface scum and reduce heat to medium. Add all the other ingredients and additional water to ensure vegetables are covered. Simmer for 3-4 hours until the liquid reduces by half, then remove from heat and strain into sterilized containers. May be frozen.

FOR POPPY SEED VINAIGRETTE: mix 2 tablespoons dry mustard with a similar quantity of warm water and blend thoroughly. Place ¹/₂ cup vinegar, 3 tablespoons puréed onion, 1 tablespoon poppy seeds, 1 teaspoon salt and 3 tablespoons sugar in a food processor and blend slowly while gradually pouring in 1 cup olive oil. Then, add the mustard and process for a further 30 seconds. Refrigerate for 2-3 hours before serving.

TO MAKE A ROUX: use 1 part bacon drippings, butter or oil to 2 or 3 parts all-purpose flour, depending on how thick a roux is desired. Mix in a heavy skillet (a cast iron skillet works best) and stir on a low heat until the roux changes from a cream to a dark chocolate colour. The cooking time can be from 30-45 minutes, depending on how dark the roux is to be. To make a white roux, add cream or milk when the colour turns to light brown. A white roux is used for soups and sauces. The slow cooking process gives the roux a nutlike flavour.

TO BOIL CRAB OR SHRIMP: place the seafood in rapidly-boiling water until it turns pink, then drain and place in 4-5 quarts of cold water with ice. Stir in 1 cup of salt, 1 teaspoon of Creole seasoning, 2 teaspoons of black pepper, 12 cloves, 1 teaspoon of Allspice, 1 teaspoon of dry mustard, 4 broken bay leaves, 1 teaspoon of thyme, 1 teaspoon of dried basil, 1 cup of fresh lemon juice and 1 teaspoon of Louisiana hot sauce. Allow to stand for 15-30 minutes, depending on how spicy the seafood is preferred.

TO MAKE CREOLE SEASONING: mix together 2 ounces of granulated garlic, 2 ounces of paprika, 2 ounces of black pepper, 1 teaspoon of cayenne pepper, teaspoon of ground oregano and 1 tablespoon of granulated onion. Store in a sealed container.

APPETIZERS

ARTICHOKE SOUFFLE SQUARES

24 ounces artichoke hearts, marinated in oil
2 cups finely chopped green onion
2 tablespoons puréed garlic
24 soda crackers
8 large eggs
1 tablespoon Creole seasoning
½ teaspoon salt
1 cup shredded Gouda cheese
2 cups sharp Cheddar cheese
1 cup seasoned breadcrumbs

Drain the oil from the marinated artichokes into a skillet and place over a medium heat. Sauté the onion for 5 minutes, then add the garlic and continue to stir for a further minute. Remove from heat and set aside. Crumble the crackers in a food processor and run until the crumbs are coarse, then transfer to a mixing bowl. Place the artichokes in the processor and chop until reasonably fine, but do not purée, then add to the bowl. Beat the eggs with the seasonings and add to the bowl, together with the onion from the skillet and the shredded cheeses. Mix thoroughly, then pour into a greased 9-inch × 12-inch baking pan and sprinkle the breadcrumbs evenly on top. Bake in a pre-heated oven (350°F) for 30-35 minutes, then remove and cut into 1-inch squares. Yields approximately 48 squares.

CAJUN PATE

³/₄ pound raw chicken livers
¹/₂ pound fresh mushrooms
3 hard boiled eggs
6 ounces butter
³/₄ cup finely chopped green onion
1 tablespoon puréed garlic

5 teaspoons lemon juice
1 teaspoon salt
¹/₂ teaspoon black pepper
³/₄ teaspoon cayenne pepper
finely chopped pecans

Place livers, mushrooms and eggs in a food processor and blend until thick and creamy. Melt the butter in a skillet and sauté the onion over a medium-high heat for 5 minutes, then add the puréed liver and continue to stir for a further 5 minutes. Add the garlic, lemon juice, salt and peppers and stir well, then remove from heat and allow to cool. Remove the mixture to a cleaned processor and blend until smooth. Line a mold with plastic wrap and fill with the paté mixture, then garnish with finely chopped pecans. Refrigerate for at least 6 hours before serving with garlic toast or crackers.

RUMAKE

¹/₂ pound raw chicken livers
10 strips bacon
6-ounce can sliced water chestnuts
3 tablespoons honey

2 tablespoons soy sauce
¹/₄ cup olive oil
2 tablespoons grenadine
2 tablespoons puréed garlic

Cut the liver into small pieces. Sauté the bacon in a little oil until half cooked, then wrap each slice around a piece of liver and water chestnut. Secure with toothpicks and place in a shallow ovenproof dish. Mix together the honey, soy sauce, olive oil, grenadine and garlic and pour over the bacon rolls. Refrigerate for 6 hours. To cook: place the dish in a pre-heated oven (350°F) for 20-25 minutes. Serve immediately. Yields approximately 20 pieces.

HOT SEAFOOD DIP

4 ounces butter

1/2 cup finely chopped yellow onion

1/2 cup finely chopped green onion

1/2 cup finely chopped celery

1/2 cup finely chopped green bell pepper

1 teaspoon puréed garlic

8 ounces cream cheese

1/2 pound crawfish tail meat

1/2 pound fresh crabmeat

1 teaspoon Creole seasoning

1 teaspoon sugar

3 tablespoons dry sherry

1/4 cup mayonnaise

1 teaspoon dry mustard

1 teaspoon Louisiana hot sauce

salt to taste

Melt the butter over a medium-high heat and sauté the onions, celery, bell pepper and garlic for approximately 5 minutes, then reduce heat and add cheese, crawfish and crabmeat. Sauté until the cheese is melted, then add the Creole seasoning, sugar, sherry, mayonnaise, mustard, hot sauce and salt. Simmer and stir until well blended. Serve with chips or crackers.

HOT SWISS CHEESE DIP

12 ounces shredded Swiss cheese

12 ounces frozen chopped onion, drained

2 cups mayonnaise

Blend the ingredients thoroughly and place in a baking dish. Bake in a pre-heated oven (350°F) for 30 minutes. Serve with garlic toast.

TORTILLA PINWHEELS

1 pound chicken breasts

1 teaspoon Creole seasoning

1 teaspoon Season All

1 teaspoon chilli powder

1 teaspoon salt

1 teaspoon black pepper

1/4 cup olive oil

8 12-inch flour tortillas

8 ounces softened cream cheese

1/4 cup finely chopped green bell pepper

1/4 cup finely chopped red bell pepper

1/2 cup finely chopped ripe olives

1/4 cup finely chopped green chilli pepper

1 teaspoon puréed garlic

1/2 teaspoon cayenne pepper

2 teaspoons Louisiana hot sauce

1 tablespoon lemon juice

Cut the chicken into 1-inch pieces and place in a shallow dish. Mix the Creole seasoning, Season All, chilli powder, salt and pepper and sprinkle over the chicken. Turn to coat thoroughly. Heat the oil in a skillet and sauté the chicken over a medium-high heat until cooked, then drain and set aside to cool. Next, place the chicken in a food processor and pulse-chop into coarse bits. Arrange the tortillas on a flat surface. Combine all the remaining ingredients in a mixing bowl and add the chicken. Blend thoroughly, then spread on the tortillas, leaving a 1-inch clean border. Roll up the tortillas and wrap firmly with plastic wrap, then refrigerate for at least 6 hours. To serve: remove from plastic wrap and cut into thin slices. Serve at room temperature. Yields approximately 60 pieces.

SPINACH STUFFED MUSHROOMS

8 ounces butter

1 cup finely chopped yellow onion

½ cup finely chopped green onion

¼ cup finely chopped celery

¼ cup finely chopped parsley

1 tablespoon puréed garlic

3 large eggs

1 teaspoon Creole seasoning

1 teaspoon Louisiana hot sauce

½ teaspoon thyme

½ teaspoon salt

1 teaspoon black pepper

1 teaspoon Accent

4 cups cooked chopped spinach

1 cup seasoned breadcrumbs

1½ cups finely grated Parmesan cheese

3 pounds fresh mushrooms

Melt the butter in a large skillet over a medium-high heat and sauté the yellow onion, green onion, celery, parsley and garlic for approximately 5 minutes, then remove from heat. Break the eggs into a mixing bowl, add the Creole seasoning, hot sauce, thyme, salt, pepper and Accent and beat lightly. Press excess water from the spinach and add to the bowl, together with the sautéed vegetables, breadcrumbs and 1 cup of Parmesan cheese. Blend thoroughly. Clean the mushrooms and remove stems, then stuff each one with the mixture. Arrange mushrooms on a baking sheet and sprinkle on the remaining cheese. Bake in a pre-heated oven (350°F) for 20-25 minutes and serve immediately.

SHRIMP & CRAB STUFFED MUSHROOMS

1 pound fresh shrimp

4 ounces butter

1/2 cup finely chopped green onion

1/4 cup finely chopped parsley

3 tablespoon flour

1/4 cup heavy whipping cream

1/2 cup seasoned breadcrumbs

2 tablespoons puréed garlic

1 teaspoon Louisiana hot sauce

2 tablespoons dry sherry

1 teaspoon salt

1 teaspoon Creole seasoning

1/2 pound crabmeat

1/2 cup finely grated Swiss cheese

2 pounds fresh mushrooms

Shell and de-vein the shrimp and chop finely. Melt the butter in a pan over a medium-high heat and sauté the onion and parsley for 5 minutes. Add the shrimp and sauté for a further 5 minutes, until the shrimp turns pink. Next, stir in the flour and follow with the cream. Add the breadcrumbs, garlic, hot sauce, sherry, salt and Creole seasoning, and mix well. Then, stir in the crabmeat and cheese and retain over heat until the cheese has melted. Clean the mushrooms and remove the stems, then stuff each one with the seafood mixture. Finally, arrange mushrooms in a baking dish and cook in a pre-heated oven (350°F) for 15-20 minutes.

CHEESE & SAUSAGE SOUFFLE

1 cup finely chopped Andouille sausage
1 tablespoon oil
6 slices white bread
1 teaspoon dry mustard
1/2 teaspoon cayenne pepper
1/4 cup grated Cheddar cheese
4 large eggs
2 cups cold milk

Fry the sausage in hot oil, then remove and allow to cool. Remove crusts and cut the bread into 1-inch squares. Place in a 1½-pint greased casserole dish and sprinkle on the mustard and pepper. Blend, then add the sausage, Parmesan and Cheddar and mix well. Beat the eggs with the milk and pour into the casserole, then cover and refrigerate for at least 2 hours. To cook: place the casserole in a water bath and bake in a pre-heated oven (350°F) for 1¼ hours. Serve immediately. Yields approximately 8 servings.

SAUSAGE & PINEAPPLE KEBABS

1½ pounds Andouille sausage
oil for frying
12 ounces butter
½ cup hard packed, dark brown sugar
20-ounce can pineapple chunks
8-ounce can sliced water chestnuts

Slice the sausage into ½-inch thick circles and fry in a small quantity of oil until browned. Add the butter and sugar and stir until the sugar has dissolved, then add the pineapple, with juice, and stir for 2-3 minutes. Remove pan from heat and allow to cool. Using toothpicks, make kebabs, each with a piece of sausage, a slice of water chestnut and a pineapple chunk. Place the kebabs in an ovenproof dish and add the butter from the pan. Re-heat and serve immediately. Yields approximately 36 pieces.

SALMON MOUSSE

16 ounce grilled salmon fillet

24 ounces softened cream cheese

4 tablespoons puréed yellow onion

1 tablespoon lemon juice

3 tablespoons horseradish

1 teaspoon puréed garlic

½ teaspoon salt

2 teaspoons white pepper

2 teaspoons Hickory Liquid Smoke

Place all the ingredients in a food processor and blend until creamy. Line the inside of a mold with plastic wrap and pour mousse into the mold, then refrigerate for at least 6 hours. Garnish with chopped pecans and serve with crackers. May also be served stuffed into cocktail tomatoes. Yields sufficient for 50-65 servings. For a smaller quantity of mousse, use individual ramekins and adjust measurements accordingly.

OYSTERS EN BROCHETTE
with White Remoulade Sauce

3 large eggs

8 ounces milk

1/2 pound all-purpose flour

2 teaspoons baking powder

2 tablespoons Creole seasoning

12 strips bacon

24 fresh oysters

vegetable oil for frying

Beat the eggs and milk together. Combine the flour, baking powder and Creole seasoning. Cut strips of bacon in half and grill until half cooked. Wrap each strip of bacon around an oyster and secure with toothpicks. Dredge in the seasoned flour, then dip in the egg-wash and, again, into the flour. Pre-heat the oil to 350°F and fry the oysters until golden, then drain on kitchen paper before serving with a side bowl of White Remoulade Sauce.

WHITE REMOULADE SAUCE

4 tablespoons mayonnaise

4 tablespoons sour cream

3 tablespoons Creole mustard

1/2 cup finely chopped green onion

1 tablespoon horseradish

2 tablespoons lemon juice

Place all the ingredients in a bowl and mix well. Refrigerate for 1 hour before serving at room temperature.

OYSTERS ROCKEFELLER

24 fresh oysters in shell

1¹/₂ pounds spinach

¹/₄ cup finely chopped green onion

3 tablespoons finely chopped parsley

1 cup shredded iceberg lettuce

1 teaspoon puréed garlic

1 teaspoon Louisiana hot sauce

¹/₄ cup Herbsainte liquer

1 tablespoon lemon juice

¹/₂ cup seasoned breadcrumbs

¹/₄ cup grated Parmesan cheese

3 ounces melted butter

Open the oysters carefully and clean the shells in salted water. Return the oysters to the shell and place on the top shelf of a pre-heated broiler for 5-6 minutes, until the edges start to curl. Remove from the broiler. Meanwhile, place the spinach, onion, parsley and lettuce in a food processor and grind to a fine texture. Then, add garlic, hot sauce, liqueur, lemon juice and all but 2 tablespoons of breadcrumbs and process until creamy. Now, top the oysters with the spinach mixture and sprinkle on cheese and remaining breadcrumbs. Return to the broiler for approximately 10 minutes, until the cheese starts to bubble, then dot with melted butter and serve immediately.

MARINATED SHRIMP & CRAWFISH

1 pound boiled shrimp, shelled and de-veined

1 pound boiled crawfish tails, shelled

1 large yellow onion

1 large green bell pepper

1 large red bell pepper

1 cup olive oil

4 tablespoons white vinegar

2 tablespoons fresh lemon juice

2 tablespoons chopped sweet pickle

1 teaspoon garlic powder

1 teaspoon black pepper

1 teaspoon Creole seasoning

1 teaspoon dry mustard

2 tablespoons finely chopped parsley

¼ cup finely chopped green onion

2 tablespoons capers

Arrange layers of shrimp, crawfish, yellow onion and bell peppers in a serving dish. Place the oil, vinegar, lemon juice, pickle, garlic powder, pepper, Creole seasoning and mustard in a saucepan and bring to the boil. Simmer for 2-3 minutes, then stir in the parsley, green onion and capers and remove from the heat. Allow to cool, then pour over the seafood and cover with foil. Refrigerate for 24 hours before serving.

SHRIMP BOURBON STREET
with Creole Orange Sauce

36 large fresh Gulf shrimp

3 eggs

12-ounce bottle beer

½ pound all-purpose flour

2 teaspoon baking powder

2 tablespoons Creole seasoning

vegetable oil for frying

Peel and de-vein the shrimp, leaving tails on. Beat the eggs with the beer. Mix together the flour, baking powder and Creole seasoning. Heat the oil in a frying pan to 350°F. Dredge the shrimp in flour, then dip in the egg-wash and, again, coat with flour. Cook in the hot oil until golden brown and crispy. Serve with a side-dish of Creole Orange Sauce.

CREOLE ORANGE SAUCE

12 ounces orange marmalade

4 tablespoons Creole mustard

3 tablespoons horseradish

1 teaspoon lemon juice

Mix all the ingredients in a food processor and refrigerate for 3 hours. Serve at room temperature.

COCONUT-BEER SHRIMP

36 large fresh Gulf shrimp
12-ounce bottle beer
3 eggs
2 teaspoons baking powder

2 tablespoons Creole seasoning
1/2 pound all-purpose flour
1 pound shredded coconut
vegetable oil for frying

Shell and de-vein the shrimp, leaving the tails on. Make a batter by mixing the beer, eggs, baking powder, Creole seasoning and half the flour. Dust the shrimp with the remaining flour and place in the batter, then roll in the coconut. Heat the oil in a large pan until very hot and deep-fry the shrimp until golden and crispy. Then, remove with a slotted spoon and drain on kitchen paper. Serve with a side-dish of Creole Orange Sauce. (See page 28).

CAJUN CAVIAR

8 ounces butter

1/2 pound crawfish tails, boiled and peeled

1 1/2 tablespoons Creole seasoning

1/2 pound fresh shrimp, shelled and
    de-veined

1/2 cup finely chopped yellow onion

1/2 cup finely chopped celery

1/2 cup finely chopped green bell pepper

2 tablespoons puréed garlic

1 1/2 tablespoons basil

1 tablespoon thyme

1 1/2 tablespoons tomato paste

1 1/2 tablespoons Worcestershire sauce

2 tablespoons flour

1 cup finely chopped green onion

1 teaspoon Louisiana hot sauce

1/4 teaspoon salt

Melt 2 ounces of butter in a large skillet over a high heat until it starts to sizzle, then add the crawfish and one-third of the Creole seasoning. Sauté for 3-4 minutes, then remove the crawfish and add another 2 ounces of butter to the pan. When the butter sizzles again add the shrimp and another one-third of the seasoning and sauté for 4-5 minutes, then remove the shrimp. Blend the crawfish and shrimp in a food processor to a fine texture, but do not purée, then remove and set aside. Put the yellow onion, celery and bell pepper in a sieve and squeeze out excess water. Add the remaining butter to the juices in the skillet and bring back to sizzling point. Next, add the yellow onion, celery, bell pepper, garlic and remaining Creole seasoning and cook for 5 minutes, stirring continuously. Then, reduce heat, add basil and thyme and cook for another 5 minutes. Now, add the crawfish-shrimp mixture, together with the tomato paste. Worcestershire sauce and flour and sauté over a medium heat for 4-5 minutes. Finally, add the green onion, hot sauce and salt and finish cooking for a further 5 minutes, stirring frequently. To serve: brush French bread slices with a melted parsley-butter and spread on the caviar.

BAYOU BOUDIN

2 tablespoons Creole seasoning

2 pounds lean pork

1½ pounds chicken livers

3 tablespoons olive oil

1 cup finely chopped yellow onion

1 tablespoon puréed garlic

1½ cups finely chopped green onion

5 cups cooked white rice

1 teaspoon salt

1 teaspoon black pepper

1 cup chicken stock

4 large eggs

4 cups seasoned breadcrumbs

vegetable oil for frying

Sprinkle half the Creole seasoning over the pork and liver. Heat the olive oil in a skillet and sauté the meat until browned, then add the yellow onion, garlic and 1 cup of green onion. Sauté for 4-5 minutes, then remove from heat and allow to cool. Grind the mixture in a meat grinder, then transfer to a mixing bowl and add cooked rice, remaining green onion, salt and pepper. Add sufficient stock to produce a workable consistency and shape into 1-inch balls. Beat the eggs lightly with the remaining Creole seasoning. Dip the meat balls into the egg-wash, then roll in breadcrumbs. Heat the vegetable oil in a pan to 350°F and deep-fry the meat balls until golden brown and crispy. Serve with a side-bowl of White Remoulade Sauce (see page 24).

Soups, Salads & Sides

Menu

Oyster & Andouille Soup 36

Oyster & Artichoke Soup 38

Mock Turtle Soup 39

Crawfish & Corn Chowder 40

Shrimp Remoulade Salad 42

Mushroom Salad 44

Seafood & Snow Pea Salad 45

Strawberry Spinach Salad 46

Bayou House Salad 46

Mardi Gras Rice 47

Cajun Dirty Rice 50

Betty Flynn's Potato Salad 51

Garlic Mashed Potato 52

Cajun Cornbread 54

Corn Pudding Casserole 54

Cheese Grits 55

Antipasto Salad 56

Muffuletta Sandwich 56

OYSTER & ANDOUILLE SOUP

½ cup vegetable oil

1 pound chopped Andouille sausage

½ cup all-purpose flour

1 cup finely chopped green onion

1 cup finely chopped celery

½ cup finely chopped parsley

4 cups seafood stock

1 teaspoon puréed garlic

2 teaspoons Louisiana hot sauce

1 quart heavy whipping cream

salt and pepper to taste

1 pint fresh oysters

Heat half the oil in a large heavy-based pan and sauté the sausage until well-browned, then remove the sausage and set aside. Add the remaining oil to the pan and stir in the flour. Cook over a medium heat for 20-25 minutes, stirring continuously, to make a light brown roux. Then, add the onion, celery and parsley and stir for 4-5 minutes. Stir in the stock, a cup at a time, and add the garlic, hot sauce and cream. Season with salt and pepper, reduce heat to low and allow to simmer for 25-30 minutes. Next, poach the oysters in their own juices for 4-5 minutes, until the edges begin to curl, then place two oysters into the bottom of each individual soup bowl. Add the oyster juices to the stock, together with the sausage and stir for 2 minutes, then ladle into the bowls. Yields 8-10 servings.

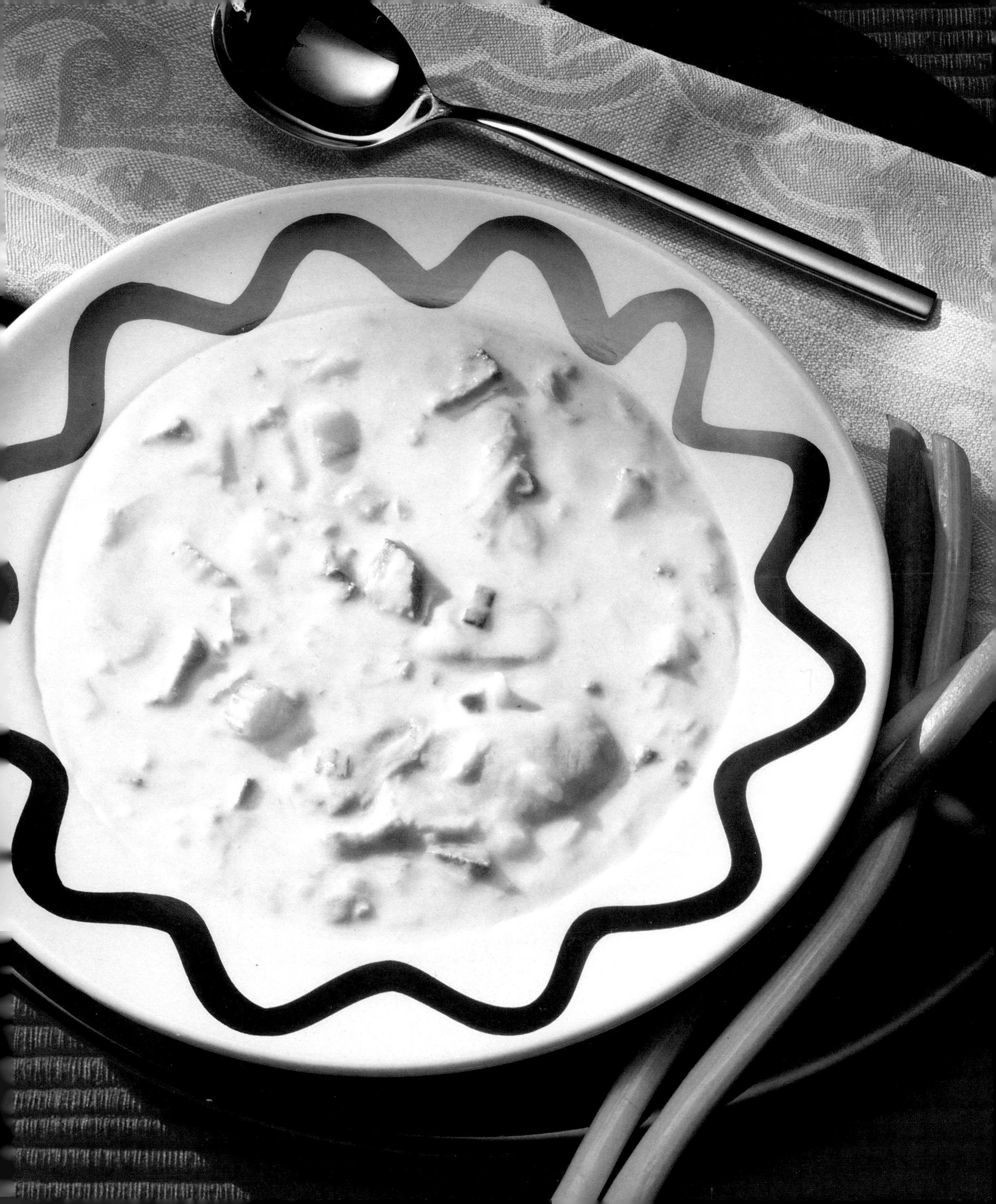

OYSTER & ARTICHOKE SOUP

4 ounces butter

¹/₂ cup finely chopped green onion

¹/₂ cup finely chopped celery

2 teaspoons puréed garlic

2 tablespoons flour

3 cups chicken stock, or clam juice

2 cups chopped artichoke hearts

2 tablespoons finely chopped parsley

2 bay leaves

1 teaspoon Creole seasoning

¹/₂ teaspoon dried thyme

¹/₂ teaspoon Louisiana hot sauce

¹/₂ teaspoon salt

¹/₂ teaspoon black pepper

24 fresh oysters

Melt half the butter in a large saucepan and sauté the onion, celery and garlic over a medium-high heat for 4-5 minutes, then stir in the flour and cook for a further 5 minutes. Pour in the stock, or clam juice, and whisk until smooth, then add artichoke, parsley, bay leaves, Creole seasoning, thyme, hot sauce, salt and pepper. Stir well and bring to the boil, then reduce heat and let simmer for 30 minutes. Next, remove the bay leaves, add the oysters and continue to simmer for a further 4-5 minutes, or until the oysters begin to curl. Serve immediately. Yields 8-10 servings.

MOCK TURTLE SOUP

½ cup vegetable oil

½ pound finely chopped beef

½ pound finely chopped pork

½ cup all-purpose flour

1 cup finely chopped yellow onion

¼ cup finely chopped celery

½ cup finely chopped green onions

½ cup finely chopped parsley

2 quarts chicken stock

6-ounce can tomato paste

1 teaspoon puréed garlic

1 teaspoon Louisiana hot sauce

salt and pepper to taste

dry sherry

2 tablespoons chopped hard-boiled egg

Heat the oil in a large, heavy-based skillet and sauté the beef and pork over a medium heat until well browned, then remove the meat and set aside. Add the flour to the skillet and stir to make a dark roux (see page 9). Add the vegetables and stir until the yellow onion is transparent, then transfer to a large saucepan. Add 1 cup of stock and the tomato paste and stir well, then add the remaining stock, a cup at a time. Add the cooked meat, garlic, hot sauce, salt and pepper and stir well. Cover the pan, reduce heat to low and simmer for 2 hours, stirring occasionally. To serve: ladle into individual bowls, add a dash of sherry and garnish with a little chopped egg.

CRAWFISH & CORN CHOWDER

8 ounces butter

½ cup finely chopped green onion

½ cup finely chopped celery

1 teaspoon puréed garlic

2 tablespoons all-purpose flour

2 cups chicken stock

1 tablespoon finely chopped parsley

1 teaspoon Creole seasoning

½ teaspoon Louisiana hot sauce

1 teaspoon salt

1 teaspoon pepper

¾ pound cooked crawfish tail meat

2 cups fresh shucked corn

2 cups heavy cream

Melt half the butter in a large saucepan and sauté the onion, celery and garlic over a medium-high heat for 4-5 minutes, then stir in the flour and cook for a further 3-4 minutes. Add the stock and whisk until smooth, then add parsley, Creole seasoning, hot sauce, salt and pepper, and bring to the boil. Reduce heat and let simmer for 30 minutes, then add the crawfish, corn and cream and continue to simmer for 10-12 minutes, until a desired consistency is reached. Finally, whisk in tablespoon measures of the remaining butter and stir to blend thoroughly. Transfer to a soup tureen and serve immediately.

SHRIMP REMOULADE SALAD

36 medium-size boiled shrimp
6 cups shredded iceberg lettuce
large tomatoes, quartered
hard-boiled eggs, quartered

Dressing:
2 tablespoons Creole mustard
1 tablespoon paprika
2 tablespoons horseradish
2 teaspoons Worcestershire sauce

1 teaspoon Louisiana hot sauce
1 teaspoon salt
1/2 teaspoon sugar
1/2 cup finely chopped green onion
1/2 cup finely chopped celery
1/2 cup finely chopped bell pepper
2 tablespoons finely chopped parsley
1/2 cup tarragon vinegar
2 cups corn oil

Place all the dressing ingredients, excluding the corn oil, in a food processor and pulsate for 3-4 seconds, then add the oil in a steady stream while the processor is running. Pour the dressing over the shrimp and marinate in the refrigerator for 3-4 hours. To serve: arrange 6 beds of lettuce on individual serving plates and top with the shrimp. Garnish with egg and tomato.

MUSHROOM SALAD

2 tablespoons unsalted butter

3/4 pound fresh mushrooms, quartered

1 large ripe tomato

1/2 teaspoon sugar

1/2 teaspoon salt

1/2 cup finely chopped red onion

3 tablespoons finely chopped green onion

2 tablespoons finely chopped parsley

Dressing:

1/3 cup heavy whipping cream

1 tablespoon white wine vinegar

1 tablespoon Creole mustard

2 tablespoons olive oil

Melt the butter in a skillet and sauté the mushrooms over a medium-heat for approximately 1 minute, until the butter is absorbed, then remove the mushroom to a dish and allow to cool. Peel the tomato, sprinkle it with sugar and salt and let stand for 15 minutes. Then, pat the tomato dry, cut into small dice and add to the mushrooms, together with the red onion and the dressing ingredients. Toss well, then add the green onion and parsley and toss again lightly. Serve at room temperature. Yields approximately 6 servings.

To make the dressing: pour the cream into a mixing bowl and beat until thick and creamy, then whisk in the vinegar and mustard until stiff peaks form. Finally, add the oil in a steady stream, whisking continuously until thoroughly incorporated.

SEAFOOD & SNOW PEA SALAD
with Lime-Mustard Vinaigrette

20 large boiled shrimp

³/₄ pound fresh lump crabmeat

20 snow peas

10 large mushrooms, thinly sliced

¹/₂ cup finely chopped macadamia nuts

4 tablespoons finely chopped red onion

8 large lettuce leaves

Shell and de-vein the shrimp, chop coarsely and combine with the crabmeat. Blanch the snow peas in boiling water for 2-3 minutes, then transfer to a bowl of lightly-salted cold water. Next, drain the peas and slice, diagonally, into three pieces. In a large mixing bowl, combine the seafood, snow peas, mushroom, nuts and onion and pour in the prepared vinaigrette (see below). Toss gently and serve on crispy lettuce leaves.

LIME-MUSTARD VINAIGRETTE

¹/₂ cup fresh lime juice

2 tablespoons Creole mustard

2 tablespoons fresh dill, finely chopped

¹/₂ teaspoon salt

¹/₂ teaspoon black pepper

¹/₂ cup olive oil

¹/₂ cup vegetable oil

Place the lime juice, mustard, dill, salt and pepper into a food processor. Run at high speed and gradually pour in both the oils, until incorporated.

STRAWBERRY SPINACH SALAD
with Lemon Dressing

6 cups coarsely torn fresh spinach
1 pound fresh strawberriess, sliced
1 cup chopped walnuts

Dressing:
¼ cup sugar
3 tablespoons fresh lemon juice
1 large egg yolk
6 tablespoons vegetable oil

Rinse and drain the spinach. Arrange on serving plates and top with strawberries and walnuts. Serve with a lemon dressing. To make the dressing: combine the sugar, lemon juice and egg yolk in a mixing bowl. Slowly add the oil, whisking continuously until a thick and creamy consistency has been achieved. Refrigerate for 1 hour before using.

BAYOU HOUSE SALAD
with Poppy Seed Vinaigrette

mandarin orange segments
chopped roasted pecans

greenleaf lettuce
freshly ground black pepper

Place the segments of orange over a bed of greenleaf lettuce and top with chopped pecans. Add the vinaigrette dressing (see page 9) and season with freshly ground black pepper.

MARDI GRAS RICE

8 cups cooked rice

1 cup corn

1 cup frozen peas

1/4 cup chopped green onion

3 tablespoons finely chopped parsley

1/3 cup finely chopped green bell pepper

1 1/2 cups shredded purple cabbage

1 cup mayonnaise

1 teaspoon garlic salt

2 teaspoons Creole seasoning

1 teaspoon black pepper

Combine the rice and vegetables in a mixing bowl and blend well. Mix the mayonnaise and seasonings and add to the rice. Blend gently and refrigerate for 4 hours before serving. Yields 12-16 servings.

> Mardi Gras, or 'Fat Tuesday' is the day before the start of Lent and is the culmination of celebrations and parties that have been taking place in New Orleans for many weeks. This salad is so named because it incorporates the official colours of Mardi Gras; purple, green and gold.

CAJUN DIRTY RICE

1 pound chicken gizzards

½ pound lean pork

½ pound chicken livers

⅓ cup olive oil

2 cups finely chopped yellow onion

½ cup finely chopped green bell pepper

½ cup finely chopped celery

¼ cup finely chopped green onion

2 tablespoons puréed garlic

2 teaspoons Creole seasoning

½ teaspoon cayenne pepper

2 teaspoons salt

1 teaspoon black pepper

3 tablespoons finely chopped parsley

3 cups cooked white rice

Grind the gizzards and pork in a meat grinder. Heat the oil in a large skillet and sauté the ground meat and livers until browned. Remove the livers and chop coarsely, then return to the pan, together with the vegetables and garlic. Sauté for a further 5 minutes, then add the seasonings and stir well. Remove pan from the heat, add the parsley and rice and blend thoroughly. Yields 4-6 servings.

BETTY FLYNN'S POTATO SALAD

2¹/₂ pounds medium-size red potatoes

1 cup finely chopped green onion

1 cup finely chopped celery

6 coarsley chopped boiled eggs

1 cup sweet pickle relish

1¹/₄ cups mayonnaise

1 teaspoon Creole mustard

1 teaspoon Creole seasoning

1¹/₂ teaspoons salt

1 teaspoon black pepper

4 teaspoons celery seeds

1 teaspoon Accent

Boil the potatoes for approximately 15 minutes, until a fork will easily pierce, then replace the boiling water with cold and top with ice. Allow to cool thoroughly, then drain and cut into ¹/₂-inch cubes. Blend all the remaining ingredients and stir into the potato. Cover and refrigerate for 24 hours before serving. Yields 12-16 servings.

GARLIC MASHED POTATO
with Bell Pepper Coulie

4¹/₂ pounds potatoes

8 ounces butter

8 ounces softened cream cheese

1 tablespoon puréed garlic

2 tablespoons chopped chives

¹/₂ cup heavy whipping cream

2 teaspoons salt

1 teaspoon white pepper

¹/₂ cup chopped red bell pepper

¹/₂ cup chopped green bell pepper

Peel and dice the potatoes, and place in a pot. Cover with water and bring to the boil. Boil for 15-20 minutes, then remove, drain and place in a mixer. Add 6 ounces of butter and blend on medium speed, then reduce speed and add the cream cheese, garlic, chives, cream, salt and pepper. Blend well until the potato is fluffy. Meanwhile, sauté the red and green bell peppers in the remaining butter for 4-5 minutes, then remove and drain. To serve: transfer the potato to a large bowl and garnish with the bell pepper coulie.

CAJUN CORNBREAD

2 large eggs

1 cup buttermilk

1 cup corn oil

1¾ cups yellow cornmeal

1 tablespoon baking powder

½ teaspoon baking soda

1 teaspoon salt

1 teaspoon cayenne pepper

¾ cup grated sharp Cheddar cheese

¼ cup finely chopped jalapeno pepper

¼ cup finely chopped pimento

½ cup finely chopped yellow onion

10-ounce can creamed corn

Beat the eggs, buttermilk and corn oil in a large mixing bowl and stir in all the remaining ingredients. Blend thoroughly, then pour into a well-greased cast iron skillet and bake in a pre-heated oven (350°F) for 25-30 minutes.

CORN PUDDING CASSEROLE

16-ounce can cream-style corn

2 large eggs, beaten

1 tablespoon all-purpose flour

½ cup heavy whipping cream

1 tablespoon sugar

½ teaspoon salt

1 tablespoon melted butter

Grease a 1-quart casserole dish. Mix the corn, eggs and flour in a bowl, then stir in the cream and add the sugar, salt and butter. Blend mixture thoroughly, then transfer to a greased 1-quart casserole dish. Place the dish in a pre-heated oven (350°F) and bake for 1¼ hours, until the pudding is slightly puffy and lightly browned. Yields 4-6 servings.

CHEESE GRITS

2 cups yellow corn grits

1 teaspoon salt

1 cup grated sharp Cheddar cheese

1 tablespoon puréed garlic

6 ounces butter

¼ cup heavy whipping cream

2 large eggs, beaten

Boil the grits in 6 cups of salted water for 5 minutes, then stir in the cheese, garlic, butter, cream and eggs. When the cheese is melted pour the mixture into a well-greased 9-inch x 12-inch baking pan and bake in a pre-heated oven (350°F) for 30-35 minutes.

Grits are the medium-ground grains of dried corn which, many would say, are an essential component of any true Southern breakfast. When more coarsely ground they are known as hominy grits.

ANTIPASTO SALAD
for Muffuletta Sandwich

8 ounces fresh mushrooms

4 ounces artichoke hearts

8 ounces Spanish olives

¼ cup finely chopped green bell pepper

½ cup finely chopped celery

4 ounces cocktail onions

⅔ cup white vinegar

⅔ cup olive oil

1 tablespoon Italian seasoning

1 teaspoon puréed garlic

1 teaspoon puréed yellow onion

1 teaspoon Accent

1 teaspoon black pepper

Place the mushrooms, artichoke and olives in a food processor and run slowly to produce a fine consistency, but do not purée. Transfer the mixture to a bowl and combine with the bell pepper, celery and cocktail onions. Place the remaining ingredients in a saucepan and bring to the boil. Boil for 2-3 minutes, then add to the bowl and stir to mix thoroughly. Set aside to cool, then refrigerate for 24 hours.

MUFFULETTA SANDWICH

Slice Italian cap bread, or French bread, and add layers of thinly sliced baked ham, Swiss cheese, salami and Provolone cheese. Top with a layer of Antipasto Salad and place in a medium-high oven until the cheese starts to melt. Serve immediately.

ENTREES

Menu

Shrimp Esplanade 60

Shrimp & Andouille Brochette 62

Shrimp & Andouille Pasta 63

Creole Crab Cakes 64

Creole Crabmeat Souffle 66

Bayou Enchiladas 67

Crawfish Etouffee 68

Seafood Gumbo 70

Eggplant Lagniappe 72

Pasta Jambalaya 74

Parmesan Chicken 75

Chicken Clemenceau 76

Chicken Lacombe 78

Chicken & Sausage Jambalaya 79

Creole Cordon Bleu 80

Monday's Feast (Red Beans & Rice) 82

Grillades & Grits 84

Pork Tenderloin Moutarde 86

Stuffed Smoked Pork Tenderloin 87

Creole Lasagna 88

SHRIMP ESPLANADE

24 large fresh shrimp

12 ounces butter

1 tablespoon puréed garlic

2 tablespoons Worcestershire sauce

1 teaspoon dried thyme pepper

1 teaspoon dried rosemary

1/2 teaspoon dried oregano

1/2 teaspoon crushed red pepper

1 teaspoon cayenne pepper

1 teaspoon black pepper

8 ounces beer

4 cups cooked white rice

1/2 cup finely chopped green onion

Wash the shrimp and leave in the shell. Melt the butter in a large frying pan and stir in the garlic, Worcestershire sauce and seasonings. Add the shrimp and shake the pan to immerse the shrimp in butter, then sauté over a medium-high heat for 4-5 minutes, until they turn pink. Next, pour in the beer and stir for a further minute, then remove from the heat. Shell and de-vein the shrimp and arrange on a bed of rice. Pour the pan juices on top and garnish with chopped green onion. Serve immediately.

SHRIMP & ANDOUILLE BROCHETTE
with Creole Mustard Sauce

20 large fresh shrimps

1 pound Andouille sausage

1 large yellow onion

1 large green bell pepper

1 large red bell pepper

16 ounces butter

2 tablespoons Creole seasoning

4 cups cooked white rice

¼ cup finely chopped green onion

Shell and de-vein the shrimp and cut the sausage into ½-inch thick pieces. Cut the onion and bell peppers into 1-inch pieces and sauté in 4 ounces of butter for 5-6 minutes. Alternate on lightly-oiled wooden skewers: shrimp, pepper, sausage and onion and sprinkle with Creole seasoning. Place on a medium-hot grill and cook, basting frequently with the remaining butter, until the shrimp is pink and tender. To serve: arrange brochettes on a bed of rice, top with Creole Mustard Sauce (see page 7) and garnish with chopped green onion.

SHRIMP & ANDOUILLE PASTA
with Butter Sauce

24 fresh jumbo shrimp

2 tablespoons Creole seasoning

8 ounces butter

¹/₂ pound finely chopped Andouille sausage

Butter Sauce:

16 ounces softened butter

2 tablespoons puréed garlic

1 tablespoon diced pimento

2 teaspoons capers

2 tablespoons finely chopped parsley

1 teaspoon dried thyme

1 teaspoon dried basil

¹/₂ teaspoon dried oregano

1 teaspoon Creole seasoning

salt and pepper to taste

2 teaspoon Dijon mustard

¹/₂ cup heavy whipping cream

1 teaspoon lemon juice

Shell and de-vein the shrimp. Sprinkle Creole seasoning over the shrimp and set aside for 15 minutes. Melt the butter in a skillet and sauté the shrimp and sausage over a medium-high heat for 3-5 minutes, until the shrimp turns pink. To serve: arrange on top of a preferred pasta and cover with Butter Sauce.

To make the sauce: place the softened butter in a bowl and add garlic, pimentos, capers, parsley, dry seasonings and mustard. Blend thoroughly but do not beat. Roll the butter into a log, wrap in wax paper and refrigerate for at least 24 hours. Then pour the cream into a saucepan and bring to the boil. Add tablespoon pieces of the cold butter and stir until melted and a desired consistency has been reached, then remove from the heat and stir in the lemon juice. Serve immediately.

CREOLE CRAB CAKES
with Creole Tomato Sauce and Jalapeno Tarter Sauce

1 pound fresh lump crabmeat

1/4 cup finely chopped green onion

2 tablespoons finely chopped yellow onion

2 tablespoons finely chopped green bell pepper

1/4 cup grated Romano cheese

1/2 cup seasoned breadcrumbs

1 teaspoon puréed garlic

1/2 cup mayonnaise

1 large egg, lightly beaten

1 tablespoon Worcestershire sauce

1 teaspoon Louisiana hot sauce

1/2 teaspoon thyme

2 teaspoons Creole seasoning

salt to taste

8 ounces butter

Combine all the ingredients, excluding the butter, in a mixing bowl and shape into 2-inch balls. Roll in additional seasoned breadcrumbs, then flatten with the hands to produce 1/2-inch thick patties. To cook: heat the butter in a large skillet and fry the patties over a medium-high heat until golden on both sides. Serve on a bed of Jalapeno Tarter Sauce with a side-dish of hot Creole Tomato Sauce (see pages 7 and 8).

CREOLE CRABMEAT SOUFFLE

4 ounces butter

1 cup finely chopped yellow onion

½ cup finely chopped green bell pepper

1 cup finely chopped green onion

1 cup sliced mushrooms

12 slices white bread, crusts removed

1 cup shredded sharp Cheddar cheese

1 cup shredded Parmesan cheese

1 pound lump crabmeat

1 teaspoon salt

1 teaspoon white pepper

10 large eggs

3 cups milk

1 teaspoon Louisiana hot sauce

¼ cup dry white wine

1 tablespoon Worcestershire sauce

1 tablespoon Creole seasoning

Melt the butter in a large skillet and sauté the yellow onion, bell pepper, green onion and mushroom on a medium-high heat for 5-6 minutes, then remove from the heat and set aside. Cut the bread into 1-inch squares and line the bottom of a 3-quart baking dish. Spread the sautéed mixture on the bread, add a layer of cheeses, top with crabmeat and season with salt and pepper. Next, break the eggs into a mixing bowl and beat lightly together with the milk, hot sauce, wine, Worcestershire sauce and Creole seasoning, then pour into the pan. Refrigerate for at least 4 hours. To cook: place pan in a pre-heated oven (325°F) and bake for 1 hour. Serve immediately. Yields 6-8 servings.

BAYOU ENCHILADAS
with Creole Tomato Sauce

4 ounces unsalted butter

1/2 cup finely chopped bell pepper

1 1/2 cups finely chopped yellow onion

6 ounces cream cheese

2 cups heavy whipping cream

1/2 pound cooked crawfish tail meat

1/4 cup finely chopped green onion

1 cup finely chopped chilli pepper

1/4 teaspoon chopped cilantro

1/2 teaspoon chilli powder

1/4 teaspoon cumin

1/2 teaspoon salt

1/2 teaspoon black pepper

2 cups grated Monterey Jack cheese

1/2 cup grated jalapeno pepper cheese

1 cup vegetable oil

8 10-inch corn tortillas

2 cups Creole Tomato Sauce (see page 7)

2 cups grated mozzarella cheese

Melt the butter in a large saucepan and sauté the bell pepper and yellow onion for 4-5 minutes, then add the cream cheese and cream and allow to simmer for 8-10 minutes, stirring frequently. Next, add the crawfish, green onion, chilli pepper and seasonings, and blend well. Remove pan from heat and stir in the cheeses. Allow to cool, then refrigerate until the mixture is firm. Heat the oil in a pan. Holding the tortillas with tongs, dip into the oil for a few seconds, then drain on kitchen paper. Place 3 tablespoons of the crawfish mixture on each tortilla, then roll and place in a baking dish with the seam side down. Cover with the tomato sauce and sprinkle the mozzarella on top. Place under a broiler until the cheese starts to bubble, then serve immediately.

CRAWFISH ETOUFFEE

3 ounces butter

1/4 cup all-purpose flour

1 cup finely chopped yellow onion

3/4 cup finely chopped green bell pepper

1/2 cup finely chopped celery

4 teaspoons puréed garlic

1 pound cooked crawfish tail meat

3 tablespoons finely chopped parsley

2 teaspoons lemon juice

1/4 teaspoon thyme

1/2 teaspoon basil

1/4 teaspoon paprika

1/4 teaspoon cayenne pepper

1/2 teaspoon white pepper

1/2 teaspoon black pepper

1/4 teaspoon salt

1 cup finely chopped green onion

1 cup seafood stock (see page 8)

Melt the butter in a heavy iron pot over a low heat and stir in the flour. Using a whisk, stir continuously to produce a light brown roux (see page 9). Increase the heat to medium, add the yellow onion, bell pepper, celery and garlic and sauté for 12-15 minutes, until the onion is translucent. Next, add the crawfish, parsley, lemon juice, seasonings and all but 2 tablespoons of the green onion. Stir well, then pour in the stock and bring to the boil. Finally, lower heat and simmer for 15 minutes, stirring frequently, to reduce stock. Serve on a bed of rice and garnish with the remaining chopped green onion.

SEAFOOD GUMBO

½ cup all-purpose flour

½ cup olive oil

½ cup finely chopped celery

1 cup finely chopped yellow onion

¾ cup finely chopped bell pepper

1 tablespoon puréed garlic

2 teaspoons Louisiana hot sauce

¼ tablespoon thyme

¼ teaspoon oregano

¼ teaspoon cayenne pepper

½ teaspoon salt

¼ teaspoon white pepper

¼ teaspoon black pepper

¾ cup chopped tomato

6 cups seafood stock (see page 8)

½ pound okra, cut into ½-inch slices

½ pound coarsley chopped Andouille sausage

½ pound shrimp, shelled and de-veined

1 tablespoon file

Place the flour and half the oil in a cast iron Dutch oven and make a dark brown roux (see page 9). Then, add celery, onion and bell pepper and cook until tender. Add the garlic and all seasonings and stir for 5 minutes, then add tomato and stock and bring to the boil. Lower heat and let simmer for 15 minutes. Meanwhile, heat the remaining oil in a skillet and sauté the okra for 10-12 minutes, then add to the pot and cook for a further 5 minutes. Add the sausage and shrimp. Mix the file with a tablespoon of warm water and stir the resulting paste into the gumbo. Continue to simmer for a further 30-40 minutes, stirring occasionally. Serve in bowls with white rice. Yields 6-8 servings.

File is the powder from ground sassafras leaves which is used to help thicken soups and stews (gumbos) and to add a slightly lemon-scented flavor.

EGGPLANT LAGNIAPPE
with Seafood Butter Sauce

6 cups eggplant, in ½-inch cubes

salt

12 ounces butter

½ cup finely chopped yellow onion

½ cup finely chopped green bell pepper

½ cup finely chopped celery

½ pound coarsley chopped Andouille
    sausage

1 tablespoon Italian seasoning

1 teaspoon sage

½ cup finely chopped green onion

2 cups cooked white rice

1 large eggplant, cut in ¼-inch slices

¾ cup flour

4 eggs, beaten

1 cup seasoned breadcrumbs

vegetable oil for frying

Place the diced eggplant in a colander and sprinkle lightly with salt. Set aside for 1 hour, then rinse and drain thoroughly. Melt 8 ounces of butter in a large frying pan and sauté the eggplant over a medium-high heat for 8-10 minutes until tender but not mushy. Then, remove eggplant and set aside. Melt the remaining butter in the pan juices and sauté the yellow onion, bell pepper and celery for 5-6 minutes, until the onion becomes translucent, then add the sausage, Italian seasoning and sage and cook for a further 5 minutes, stirring frequently. Return the sautéed eggplant to the pan, together with the green onion and rice and stir to blend thoroughly. Next, coat the sliced eggplant with flour, then dip into the beaten eggs and roll in breadcrumbs. Fry in hot oil until golden, then, drain on kitchen paper and arrange on a serving plate. Add a portion of sautéed eggplant mixture to each slice of eggplant and top with Seafood Butter Sauce (see page 7).

PASTA JAMBALAYA

14 ounces butter

³/₄ cup finely chopped yellow onion

¹/₂ cup finely chopped green bell pepper

¹/₄ cup finely chopped red bell pepper

1 tablespoon puréed garlic

20 ounces raw chicken meat,
  in bite-size pieces

8 ounces coarsely chopped Andouille
  sausage

8 ounces cooked duck breast,
  in bite-size pieces

12 ounces chicken stock (see page 9)

2 cups peeled and diced tomatoes

1 tablespoon Creole seasoning

¹/₂ teaspoon red pepper flakes

12 medium-size shrimp, shelled
  and de-veined

6 cups cooked linguini

1 cup finely chopped green onion

Heat 6 ounces of butter in a skillet and sauté the yellow onion, bell peppers and garlic over a medium-high heat for approximately 5 minutes, then add the chicken and sausage and continue to sauté for a further 5 minutes, until the chicken is tender. Next, add the duck, stock, tomato and seasonings and stir for another 5 minutes, until the stock has reduced by one-third. Add the shrimp and swirl in the remaining butter, a tablespoon at a time. Remove from the heat when the shrimps turn pink and the butter has melted. To serve: ladle the mixture over hot linguini and garnish with chopped green onion. Yields 6 servings.

PARMESAN CHICKEN

1 cup grated Parmesan cheese

¹/₂ cup seasoned breadcrumbs

3 tablespoons finely chopped parsley

1 tablespoon paprika

1 teaspoon garlic powder

1 tablespoon oregano

1 teaspoon black pepper

6 boned and skinned chicken breasts

8 ounces melted butter

Combine the cheese, breadcrumbs, parsley, paprika, garlic powder, oregano and pepper and blend well. Dredge the chicken breasts in melted butter, then place in the cheese mixture, turning to coat evenly. Place the breasts in a baking pan and cook in a pre-heated oven (350°F) for 25-30 minutes. Serve on a bed of chosen pasta.

CHICKEN CLEMENCEAU

6 boned chicken breasts
1 pound Andouille sausages
12 ounces butter
3 tablespoons puréed garlic
12 ounces sliced mushroom
8 ounces small green peas
1 teaspoon salt
vegetable oil for frying
4 cups diced white potato

Cut the chicken and sausages into bite-size pieces. Heat 2 ounces of butter in a skillet and brown the sausage, then add the remaining butter and garlic and stir until the butter melts. Increase the heat to medium-high and add the chicken. Sauté for 5-6 minutes, until the chicken is three-quarters cooked, then add the mushroom, peas and salt and continue to stir until the mushroom is tender. Meanwhile, heat the oil in a pan until very hot and fry the diced potato until golden, then drain off the excess oil and add the potato to the chicken. Stir well and serve immediately.

CHICKEN LACOMBE

2 tablespoons butter

¹/₂ cup sliced mushroom

¹/₂ cup finely chopped green onion

¹/₂ pound cooked crawfish tail meat

³/₄ cup heavy whipping cream

1 teaspoon brandy

¹/₂ teaspoon chopped dill

¹/₂ teaspoon salt

¹/₂ teaspoon cayenne pepper

1 tablespoon Creole seasoning

4 boned and skinned chicken breasts

Melt the butter in a saucepan and sauté the mushroom and onion for approximately 5 minutes. Then, add the crawfish and 1 cup of water and simmer until the liquid has evaporated. Stir in the cream, add the brandy, dill, salt and pepper and cook on a medium heat, stirring frequently, for 5-6 minutes, until the sauce starts to thicken. Sprinkle Creole seasoning over the chicken and cook over charcoal until tender, then transfer to a serving platter and top with the crawfish sauce.

CHICKEN & SAUSAGE JAMBALAYA

¹/₂ cup vegetable oil

3¹/₂ pounds chicken, cut into pieces

2 cups finely chopped yellow onion

¹/₂ cup finely chopped green bell pepper

1 cup finely chopped green onion

¹/₄ cup finely chopped parsley

1 tablespoon puréed garlic

1 pound coarsely diced Andouille sausage

1 teaspoon salt

1 teaspoon black pepper

¹/₂ teaspoon chilli powder

¹/₂ teaspoon cayenne powder

¹/₄ teaspoon thyme

¹/₄ teaspoon basil

4 cups chicken stock (see page 9)

2 cups long-grain white rice

1 cup finely diced tomato

Heat the oil in a large iron pot and cook the chicken over a high heat until tender. Then, remove the chicken, cut the meat from the bones and set aside. Add the vegetables, parsley, garlic and sausage to the pan juices and sauté for 8-10 minutes. Then, add the seasonings and continue to cook for a further 5 minutes, stirring frequently. Next add the stock and rice and bring to the boil, then reduce heat. Cover the pot and cook slowly for approximately 40 minutes, stirring occasionally, until the stock reduces and the Jambalaya is soft but not soupy. Finally, add the chicken meat and tomato and stir for 5 minutes. Serve immediately. Yields 6-8 servings.

Jambalaya is a culinary contribution from the early Spanish settlers in southern Louisiana and might well be called Cajun Paella. Chilli powder, used in this recipe, is an infrequent ingredient in Creole and Cajun cooking.

CREOLE CORDON BLEU

6 boned and skinned chicken breasts

3 tablespoons Creole seasoning

¼ cup olive oil

1½ cups grated Parmesan cheese

6 cups cooked white rice

½ cup finely diced Tasso (Cajun smoked ham)

¼ cup finely chopped green onion

2 cups heavy whipping cream

1 teaspoon black pepper

4 ounces cold butter

Coat the chicken with Creole seasoning. Heat the oil and sauté the chicken, on a high heat, for 6-7 minutes, turning once. Transfer the chicken to a baking tray and place in a pre-heated oven (350°F) for approximately 5 minutes. Then, place the chicken breasts on a bed of cooked rice, sprinkle the Parmesan cheese on top and put under a broiler until the cheese melts. Meanwhile, place the Tasso, onion, cream and pepper in a saucepan and bring to the boil. Retain on a low boil for 5-6 minutes to reduce, then whisk in the butter, a tablespoon at a time. Finally, add the remaining cheese and stir until melted, then pour sauce over the chicken. Serve immediately.

MONDAY'S FEAST
(New Orleans' Red Beans & Rice)

1 pound red kidney beans

3 pounds ham hocks

6 bay leaves

2 cups coarsley chopped yellow onion

2 cups coarsley chopped celery

1 cup coarsley chopped green bell pepper

2 tablespoons puréed garlic

3 tablespoons Worcestershire sauce

2 teaspoons Louisiana hot sauce

½ teaspoon thyme

½ teaspoon oregano

1 tablespoon salt

1 teaspoon cayenne pepper

1 teaspoon white pepper

1 teaspoon black pepper

6 ounces cold butter, cut into small pieces

8 cups cooked white rice

½ cup finely chopped green onion

Soak the beans in cold water for at least 12 hours. Boil the ham hocks in 2 gallons of water until the meat falls off the bone. Remove bones from the stock and skim off the surface fat. Then, add the pre-soaked beans and the bay leaves and cook over a medium-high heat for approximately 2 hours. Add the yellow onion, celery, bell pepper, garlic and seasonings and cook for a further 25 minutes, then discard bay leaves. Finally, swirl in small pieces of cold butter and transfer to a large dish. Serve on a bed of rice and garnish with chopped green onion. Serve side plates of Cajun Cornbread (see page 54).

> In the early days in New Orleans, Monday was the traditional wash-day so there was no time for preparing a multi-course meal and the solution was to have a pot of red beans simmering on the stove ready for the evening 'feast'.

GRILLADES & GRITS

2 pounds veal cutlets

1 cup all-purpose flour

2 tablespoons Creole seasoning

$^1/_4$ cup vegetable oil

1 cup chopped yellow onion

$^1/_2$ cup chopped bell pepper

$^1/_2$ cup chopped celery

1 tablespoon puréed garlic

1$^3/_4$ cups chopped tomato

4 tablespoons tomato paste

1 bay leaf

$^1/_2$ teaspoon basil

$^1/_2$ teaspoon thyme

$^1/_2$ teaspoon oregano

$^1/_2$ teaspoon sugar

$^1/_2$ teaspoon salt

1 teaspoon black pepper

$^1/_2$ cup red wine

1$^1/_4$ cups beef stock

2 tablespoons Worcestershire sauce

$^1/_4$ cup chopped green onion

1 tablespoon chopped parsley

Pound the cutlets with a tenderizing mallet until quite thin. Mix the flour and Creole seasoning and coat each cutlet lightly. Heat the oil in a skillet and sauté the cutlets until browned, then remove and keep warm. Add the yellow onion to the skillet together with the bell pepper, celery and garlic. Sauté over a medium-high heat for 5 minutes, then add the tomato, tomato paste, herbs, sugar, salt and pepper. Simmer for a further 5 minutes. Next, add the wine, stock, Worcestershire sauce, green onion and parsley and bring to the boil. Then, reduce heat, replace the cutlets, cover the pan and let simmer for 30-35 minutes. Remove the bay leaf and serve on a bed of hot Cheese Grits (see page 55).

PORK TENDERLOIN MOUTARDE

8 3-ounce pork tenderloins

3 tablespoons Creole mustard

1/4 cup all-purpose flour

1/2 teaspoon salt

1 teaspoon white pepper

1/2 teaspoon Creole seasoning

4 ounces butter

1/4 cup olive oil

1 cup diced Granny Smith apple

1 cup thinly sliced cucumber

1 1/2 cups Reisling wine

8 thin 3-inch square slices Gouda cheese

1/4 cup finely chopped parsley

Trim any fat from the tenderloins and pound with a smooth-surface meat mallet. Spread half the mustard on one side of each tenderloin. Combine the flour, salt, pepper and Creole seasoning and use to dust both sides of the tenderloins. Heat the butter and oil in a skillet and sauté the pork over a medium-high heat for 2-3 minutes, then remove and keep warm. Add the apple, cucumber, wine and remaining mustard to the skillet juices and cook for 5 minutes, stirring frequently, until the liquid is reduced by half. Reduce the heat, replace the pork and top each tenderloin with a slice of cheese. Cook for a further 2-3 minutes, then remove the pork. To serve: serve portions of rice on individual plates, pour on the sauce and place the meat on top. Garnish with freshly chopped parsley and serve immediately.

STUFFED SMOKED PORK TENDERLOIN
with Raisin Sauce

2 cups all-purpose flour

1 cup cornmeal

1 tablespoon baking powder

1 cup sugar

2 teaspoons salt

2 cups milk

1/2 cup melted butter

4 eggs, beaten

8 6-ounce smoked pork tenderloins

1/4 cup diced Tasso (Cajun smoked ham)

1/2 cup diced Andouille sausage

1/2 cup finely chopped yellow onion

1/2 cup finely chopped celery

1 cup chicken stock (see page 8)

Combine the flour, cornmeal, baking powder, sugar, salt, milk, butter and 2 eggs and pour into a greased baking pan. Bake in a pre-heated oven (350°F) for 15 minutes, then remove and stir in the Tasso, sausage, onion, celery and remaining eggs. Increase heat to 400°F and bake for a further 30 minutes, then remove and allow to cool. Next, trim any fat from the tenderloins and slice, lengthways, three-quarter ways across. Stuff 3-4 tablespoons of the prepared mixture into each tenderloin. Heat the oil in a large skillet and fry the pork over a medium-high heat for 5-6 minutes. Then, transfer to a large plate, top with raisin sauce (see page 8) and serve immediately.

CREOLE LASAGNA

cooked lasagna noodles

3 cups cooked spinach

1 cup Ricotta cheese

6 hard-boiled eggs, sliced

1/4 cup grated Parmesan cheese

Meat Sauce:

1/4 cup olive oil

1/2 pound chopped Andouille sausage

1 pound lean ground beef

5 cups canned peeled tomatoes, with juice

1 cup finely chopped yellow onion

1/4 cup finely chopped green bell pepper

1/2 cup finely chopped ripe olives

2 tablespoons finely chopped parsley

1 tablespoon puréed garlic

12-ounce can tomato sauce

1 cup dry red wine

1 teaspoon Worcestershire sauce

1/2 teaspoon sugar

1 tablespoon Italian seasoning

1 teaspoon Creole seasoning

1 teaspoon salt

1/2 teaspoon black pepper

1 cup grated sharp Cheddar cheese

Grease a medium-size ovenproof dish and place a layer of noodles on the bottom. Cover with a layer of meat sauce (see below), then another layer of noodles. Mix the spinach and Ricotta cheese and spread this on next, then a third layer of noodles. Add the sliced boiled eggs and ladle on more sauce, then top with a final layer of noodles. Bake in a pre-heated oven (350°F) for 30 minutes, then remove and ladle on more sauce. Top with Parmesan cheese and serve immediately.

To make the sauce: heat the oil in a skillet and sauté the sausage and beef until browned, then transfer meat and oil to a large pot. Place the tomatoes in a food processor and lightly pulsate, but do not purée. Transfer the tomato to the pot, together with all the other ingredients, excluding the cheese. Place the pot on a medium heat and simmer for 50 minutes, until the sauce is fairly thick, then add the cheese and stir until melted.

DESSERTS

CHOCOLATE DECADENCE

8 ounces butter

8 ounces unsweetened chocolate

4 ounces semi-sweet chocolate

1¹/₃ cups sugar

6 large eggs

Cut a circle of wax paper and place in the bottom of a greased 9-inch spring pan, then grease the paper. Cut the butter into small pieces and grate both chocolates. Pour ¹/₂ cup of water into a saucepan, add a cup of sugar and bring to a rapid boil. Boil for 2 minutes, then remove pan from the heat and slowly stir in the grated chocolate. Next, add the butter, stirring to dissolve completely. Place the eggs and remaining sugar in a mixing bowl and beat until the sugar dissolves, then add the chocolate mixture and blend thoroughly. Pour the mixture into the prepared pan and place in a baking tray. Pour in hot water to reach three-quarters up the side of the pan. Bake in a pre-heated oven (350°F) for 25-30 minutes, then remove pan from the water bath and place on a cooling rack. Leave for 15 minutes, then refrigerate for at least 2 hours. Cut the cake while still cold but serve at room temperature on a bed of White Chocolate Sauce.

WHITE CHOCOLATE SAUCE

1 ounce heavy whipping cream

9 ounces Toblar Narsisse, or other fine chocolate

4 ounces Drambui liqueur

Scald the cream in a saucepan. Grate the chocolate and whisk into the cream, then add the Drambui. Set aside to cool.

SARAH'S HOLIDAY COOKIES

8 ounces unsalted butter

1½ cups sugar

2 large eggs

2½ cups sifted all-purpose flour

1 teaspoon baking soda

1 teaspoon cinnamon

¼ teaspoon nutmeg

1 teaspoon salt

24 ounces chopped dates

8 ounces chopped candied cherries

8 ounces chopped candied pineapple

16 ounces chopped pecans

Have the butter at room temperature, then place in a mixer set on low speed and gradually add the sugar until thoroughly blended. Beat the eggs and add to the mixer, together with the flour, baking soda, cinnamon, nutmeg and salt and mix well. Finally, stir in the chopped fruit and nuts. To cook: drop teaspoon-size portions on to a lightly-greased cookie sheet and bake in a pre-heated oven (350°F) on the centre rack for approximately 10 minutes (take care not to overbake). Turn on to a wire rack to cool.

CHOCOLATE COOKIE BARS

4 ounces butter

1 cup Graham cracker crumbs

1 cup shredded coconut

8 ounces semi-sweet chocolate chips

6 ounces butterscotch chips

14-ounce can sweetened condensed milk

1 cup chopped pecans

Melt the butter in a 9-inch x 12 inch baking pan and sprinkle on a layer of cracker crumbs. Next, add layers, first of the shredded coconut, then of chocolate and butterscotch chips. Pour the condensed milk over all and cover with a top layer of chopped pecans. Bake in a pre-heated oven (350°F) for 30 minutes, then allow to cool and refrigerate for 2-3 hours. Cut into squares to serve.

CREOLE PRALINES

1¹/₂ cups brown sugar

1¹/₂ cups granulated sugar

1¹/₂ cups evaporated milk

1 tablespoon butter

¹/₄ teaspoon salt

1 teaspoon vanilla

2 cups chopped pecans

Mix the 2 sugars and the evaporated milk in a saucepan and cook over a medium-high heat until the mixture reaches 240°F on a candy thermometer, then add the butter and salt and stir until the butter is melted. Remove from the heat and let stand until the pan is cool enough to hold in the hand, then stir in the vanilla and pecans. Spoon tablespoons of the mixture onto wax paper and set aside to harden. Yields approximately 24 pralines.

MACADAMIA NUT CHEESECAKE

12-ounce box vanilla wafers

14 ounces macadamia nuts

1¼ cups sugar

6 ounces unsalted butter, melted

24 ounces softened cream cheese

3 large eggs

1 teaspoon vanilla

1 teaspoon lemon juice

Topping:

8 ounces sour cream

3 tablespoons sugar

1 teaspoon vanilla

1 teaspoon lemon juice

To make the crust: grind the vanilla wafers in a food processor until very fine, then remove and do likewise with macadamia nuts. Combine the wafer crumbs, nuts, ¼ cup of sugar and butter and mix well. Press a ⅓-inch layer of the mixture on the bottom and sides of a 10-inch spring-form pan and bake in a pre-heated oven (350°F) for 10 minutes. Then set aside to cool. Place the cream cheese, eggs, vanilla and lemon juice in a mixer and blend until smooth. Pour the mixture into the crust and bake in the oven (still set at 350°F) for 35 minutes, then remove. Meanwhile blend together the topping ingredients and spread on top of the cake. Increase the temperature of the oven to 500°F and replace the cake for 5 minutes, then remove and allow to cool. Finish with a chosen fruit and refrigerate for at least 8 hours before serving.

FRENCH SILK PIE

Shell:
3½ cups vanilla water crumbs
3 tablespoons granulated sugar
6 ounces melted butter

Filling:
12 ounces unsalted butter
1 pound Superfine sugar
3 1-ounce squares unsweetened chocolate
1 tablespoon vanilla
6 large eggs

To make the shell: place the vanilla water crumbs, granulated sugar and melted butter in a bowl and mix well. Firmly pat a ¼-inch layer of the mixture on to the bottom and sides of a 9-inch pie dish and bake in a pre-heated oven (350°F) for 12-15 minutes. Remove and allow to cool, then pour in the mousse filling and refrigerate for at least 6 hours. To serve: pipe on Chantilly Cream (see opposite page) and garnish with roasted almonds.

To make the filling: allow the unsalted butter to soften at room temperature, then place in a mixer. Run at slow speed and gradually add the Superfine Sugar. Meanwhile, melt the chocolate in a double boiler and allow to cool slightly, then, while still liquid, add to the butter and blend well. Add the vanilla and stop the mixer, then add 4 eggs and re-run the mixer on high sped for 2-3 minutes, until the mixture is fluffy. Stop the mixer again to add the remaining eggs, then run on high speed for a further 2 minutes.

SELINA KEY LIME PIE

9-inch pie shell
8 ounces softened cream cheese
14-ounce can condensed milk
4 large egg yolks
1/3 cup Key lime juice
fresh lime slices

Bake the pie shell in a pre-heated oven (350°F) for 15 minutes, then allow to cool. Place cream cheese in a mixer and beat until fluffy. With mixer on medium speed add the condensed milk, then the egg yolks and, finally, the lime juice. Pour the mixture into the pie shell and refrigerate for at least 4 hours. When serving, top the pie with Chantilly Cream and garnish with slices of fresh lime.

CHANTILLY CREAM

8 ounces heavy whipping cream
1 cup sugar
1 teaspoon vanilla
3 tablespoons sour cream

Place all the ingredients in a mixing bowl and beat until fluffy. Refrigerate until serving.

CRÈME BRÛLEE

4 tablespoons caramel topping

3 large eggs

3 egg yolks

3¼ cups heavy whipping cream

2 teaspoons vanilla

8 tablespoons dark brown sugar

Spoon a portion of caramel topping into the bottom of eight 6-ounce ramekins. Place whole eggs, yolks and sugar in a bowl and mix well, but do not beat. Pour the cream into a saucepan, add the vanilla and bring to a simmer, then slowly add to the egg mixture, whisking continuously. Ladle the mixture into the ramekins up to the rims and place in a baking pan, allowing a minimum of 2-inch spacings. Pour hot water into the pan to reach three-quarters up the sides of the ramekins. Place the pan in a pre-heated oven (350°F) and bake for 1 hour. Then, allow to cool and refrigerate for 4 hours. Finally, spread a tablespoon of dark brown sugar on top of each ramekin and place under a broiler until the sugar starts to bubble. Serve immediately.

SWEET POTATO PECAN PIE

1³/₄ cups mashed boiled sweet potato

½ cup honey

1 teaspoon cinnamon

½ teaspoon nutmeg

½ teaspoon salt

3 large eggs

½ cup sugar

1 teaspoon vanilla

1 cup chopped pecans

9-inch uncooked pastry pie shell

Place the sweet potato, honey, cinnamon, nutmeg and salt in a mixing bowl and blend well. Beat the eggs in a separate bowl and stir in the sugar and vanilla. Add the egg to the potato mixture and blend thoroughly, then stir in the chopped pecans. Spoon the mixture into the pie shell and bake in a pre-heated oven (350°F) for 1 hour. Remove and let cool before serving. Yields 6-8 slices.

BANANAS FOSTER

2 ripe bananas

6 ounces butter

1 cup dark brown sugar

4 ounces dark rum

4 scoops vanilla ice-cream

1 tablespoon chopped pecans

Peel the bananas and slice lengthways, then cut each section in half. Melt the butter in a skillet, add the sugar and stir until dissolved. Add the banana to the syrup and sauté for 3-4 minutes, then pour in the rum and cook for a further 2 minutes. Transfer the pieces of banana to individual dishes and add scoops of ice-cream. Pour on the hot syrup and garnish with chopped pecans. Serve immediately.

CALAS

1½ cups cooked rice

½ cup sugar

1½ cups self-raising flour

½ teaspoon salt

½ teaspoon cinnamon

½ teaspoon nutmeg

1 teaspoon vanilla

3 large eggs, beaten

¼ cup milk

vegetable oil for frying

Place the rice in a mixing bowl and add the sugar, flour, salt, cinnamon, nutmeg, vanilla, eggs and milk. Mix to blend thoroughly and shape into 1-inch balls. Heat the oil to 350°F and fry the rice balls until golden, then remove with a slotted spoon and dust with powdered sugar. Yields approximately 24 pieces.

This dish originated in the early 1800's when the Louisiana cooks would go to the French Quarter of New Orleans to sell their local specialities. The name originated from an African word for rice.

CAJUN VELVET PIE

5 cups finely ground vanilla wafer crumbs

20 ounces melted butter

¼ cup granulated sugar

1 cup smooth peanut butter

16 ounces softened cream cheese

14-ounce can condensed milk

1¼ cups confectioners sugar

16 ounces non-dairy whipped topping

½ cup semi-sweet chocolate shavings

½ cup chopped unsalted peanuts

Combine the vanilla wafer crumbs, butter and granulated sugar in a bowl and mix well. Firmly pat a ¼-inch layer of crumbs into the bottom of a 9-inch pie pan and bake in a pre-heated oven (350°F) for 12-15 minutes. Remove and allow to cool. Meanwhile, place peanut butter, cream cheese and condensed milk in a mixer and blend until creamy. Slowly add the confectioners sugar and blend well, then transfer to a mixing bowl. Gently fold in 12 ounces of whipped topping and mix until very smooth. Fill the pie shell with the mixture and place in a freezer for 20 minutes. Remove and pipe the remaining whipped topping decoratively over the pie and garnish with chocolate shavings and chopped peanuts. Place back in the freezer for 3-4 hours. Slice while still frozen and allow to defrost before serving.

This pie was created at our first restaurant by Sylvia Harbin and was instrumental, indeed conditional, on our first 'group booking' (for a party of eight!). Consequently, it became our 'trademark' dessert and was featured on the menu of all our restaurants. L.C.

CREOLE PECAN PIE

9-inch pie shell

1 large egg yolk

6¹/₂ ounces softened cream cheese

¹/₄ cup granulated sugar

3 teaspoons vanilla

¹/₄ cup dark brown sugar

¹/₂ cup corn syrup

3 large eggs, lightly beaten

1¹/₂ cups coarsely chopped pecans

Bake the pie shell in a pre-heated oven (350°F) for 15 minutes, then allow to cool. Combine the egg yolk, cream cheese, white sugar and half the vanilla and spread evenly over the bottom of the pie shell. Over a medium heat dissolve the brown sugar with the corn syrup, beaten eggs and remaining vanilla and stir in the pecans. Pour this mixture into the pie shell and place in a pre-heated oven (350°F). Bake for 55-60 minutes, then remove and allow to cool. Freeze for at least 3 hours before cutting. Serve at room temperature with Chantilly Cream (see page 99).

FROZEN MOCHA TOFFEE CAKE

5 frozen chocolate-toffee candy bars

8-10 ladyfinger pastries

2 tablespoons instant coffee

1 quart softened French vanilla ice-cream

1/2 cup heavy whipping cream

3 tablespoons white creme de cacao liqueur

Crush the frozen candy bars. Split the ladyfinger pastries and use to line the bottom and sides of a 9-inch spring-form pan. Dissolve the coffee in a tablespoon of boiling water and blend with the ice-cream and four-fifths of the crushed candy. Spoon the mixture into the pan and place in the freezer until firm, then cut into individual servings. Combine the cream and liqueur and pour over each serving, then top with the remaining crushed candy.

FUDGE PIE

8 ounces butter

3 ounces unsweetened chocolate

4 large eggs

1/3 cup all-purpose flour

1 1/4 cups sugar

1/4 teaspoon salt

1 teaspoon vanilla

1/2 cup chopped pecans

Melt the butter and chocolate in a double boiler. Beat the eggs in a bowl and stir in the flour, sugar and salt. Add the melted chocolate and vanilla and blend thoroughly, then pour the mixture into an ovenproof pie plate and top with chopped pecans. Bake in a pre-heated oven (350°F) for 40-45 minutes. Serve hot with ice-cream or whipped cream.

CARROT CAKE

2½ cups finely shredded carrot

¼ cup fresh lemon juice

12 ounces unsalted butter, melted

1¾ cups brown sugar

4 eggs

1 tablespoon vanilla

1 tablespoon grated lemon rind

2 cups whole wheat flour

2 cups all-purpose flour

3 teaspoons baking powder

½ teaspoon baking soda

1 teaspoon salt

2 teaspoons cinnamon

1 teaspoon allspice

¼ teaspoon nutmeg

¾ cup chopped pecans

Soak the shredded carrots in the lemon juice until the liquid is absorbed, then set aside. Place the butter and sugar in a mixing bowl and beat in the eggs, one at a time. Add the vanilla and lemon rind and blend well. Next, sift together the flour and all remaining dry ingredients, excluding the pecans. Repeat the sifting. In a fresh mixing bowl, arrange layers of carrot, butter and flour and repeat until everything is used up, ending with a layer of flour. Gently fold the mixture together until well blended (do not beat). To cook: transfer the mixture to a well-greased loaf pan, top with chopped pecans and bake in a pre-heated oven (350°F) for 45-50 minutes.

BAYOU BREAD PUDDING
with Hot Rum Sauce

20-ounce can crushed pineapple

8 ounces raisins

1 cup dark rum

30 ounces stale French bread

1 quart milk

6 ounces melted butter

3 large eggs

6 ounces evaporated milk

3 tablespoons vanilla

1½ cups granulated sugar

¼ cup dark brown sugar

Firstly, place the pineapple and raisins in a bowl, add the rum and set aside to marinate for 48 hours. Break up the bread and soak in the milk, then strain out excess liquid in a sieve and place the mushy bread in a mixing bowl. Drain the rum from the fruit and reserve liquid for making sauce. Add the fruit to the bread, together with the melted butter. In a separate bowl beat the eggs with the evaporated milk, vanilla and both sugars and add to the bread and fruit. Mix with a spoon until thoroughly blended. To cook: transfer the mixture to a well-greased 9-inch x 12-inch baking pan and bake in a pre-heated oven (350°F) for 30 minutes, then remove pan and stir well. Spread the pudding evenly and replace in the oven to bake for a further 40-45 minutes. Serve immediately with Hot Rum Sauce.

HOT RUM SAUCE

2 cups sugar

8 ounces butter

2 large eggs

4 ounces dark rum

reserved mariniade (see above)

Combine the sugar and butter in a double boiler. Beat the eggs, add to the pan and whisk rapidly to produce a thick consistency. Remove pan from the heat and allow to cool, then stir in the rum and reserved marinade. Re-heat before pouring over the pudding prior to serving.